Sinding makes ample use of the pedal, which effectively enhances the previously mentioned rustling quality. Be sure that no chord is blurred by sustaining even a part of the preceding chord. Keep the harmonies clear.

The work begins beautifully in an unusual manner, i.e., not on the tonic chord, but on the relative minor, which gives the piece a somewhat wistful quality. In measure 1, be sure to observe that the last note of the right-hand arpeggio is missing. Try to make the left-hand melody interesting and coherrent and perform it with enjoyment, as a cellist might bow it. Many pianists have difficulty in delineating good melodic line, and this is why even limited study of a stringed instrument is good for a pianist. Make the ascending passages, measures 4 and 8, become louder as they approach the initial note of the melody. Measure 10 requires some special attention: see that the scale ends undisturbed in C, which is very important. Let the seven-note arpeggio finish a little early so that the three consecutive C's sound clearly – the first C ends the arpeggio, the second finishes the scale melody, and the third begins the new arpeggio. Be careful and do not rush the passage; try to separate the texture mentally into melody and accompaniment. At measure 15 make the melodic 32nds and the left hand fit in exactly with the right hand. At measure 18 let the left-hand tied note fit the C in the right-hand part and the last two 32nds in the next measure also fit their right-hand counterparts; check these with the metronome. At measure 31 reverse the procedure and study the subject in the right hand; also note the C-flat in measure 37, especially if you will be playing the piece from memory.

In measures 31–32 check the group of five notes in the left hand and see how slow measures 33–34 sound in comparison; the seven-note groups of measures 40 and 42 must still be felt in two flowing pulses. One of the most frequent problems occurs in measure 49, where the dot is often neglected, thus robbing the first note of the measure, which should have, when correctly played, a curious halting effect (also true of measure 53). The brief cadenza-like passage at measures 45–46 may be rather broad and a little bit "stretched." Slide the fifth finger (tied note) at measures 50 and 54 over to the fourth, and notice that, in spite of all the naturals in measure 51, it is a G minor chord. The middle section begins at measure 47 with the ascending four-measure sequence, repeats a note higher at 51, and partially repeats at measure 55. Each should increase in dynamics till the crashing *fortissimo* notes at measure 57. Notice the continued presence of the dominant A-flat in each chord, right and left, measures 57 through 60. At measure 61, be sure to hold the pedal for four measures, and perhaps a small ritard at measure 64 is appropriate to show the return of the first subject. Compare measures 31 and 91, where the downward leap is shortened; this is important, again, especially if you will be playing from memory.

This form is ternary:

A = measures 1–46; B = 47–64; A = 65–98; Coda = 99–109.

Maurice Hinson

RUSTLES OF SPRING

Frühlingsrauschen

1896

Agitato (♩ =ca. 80)

Op. 32, No. 3

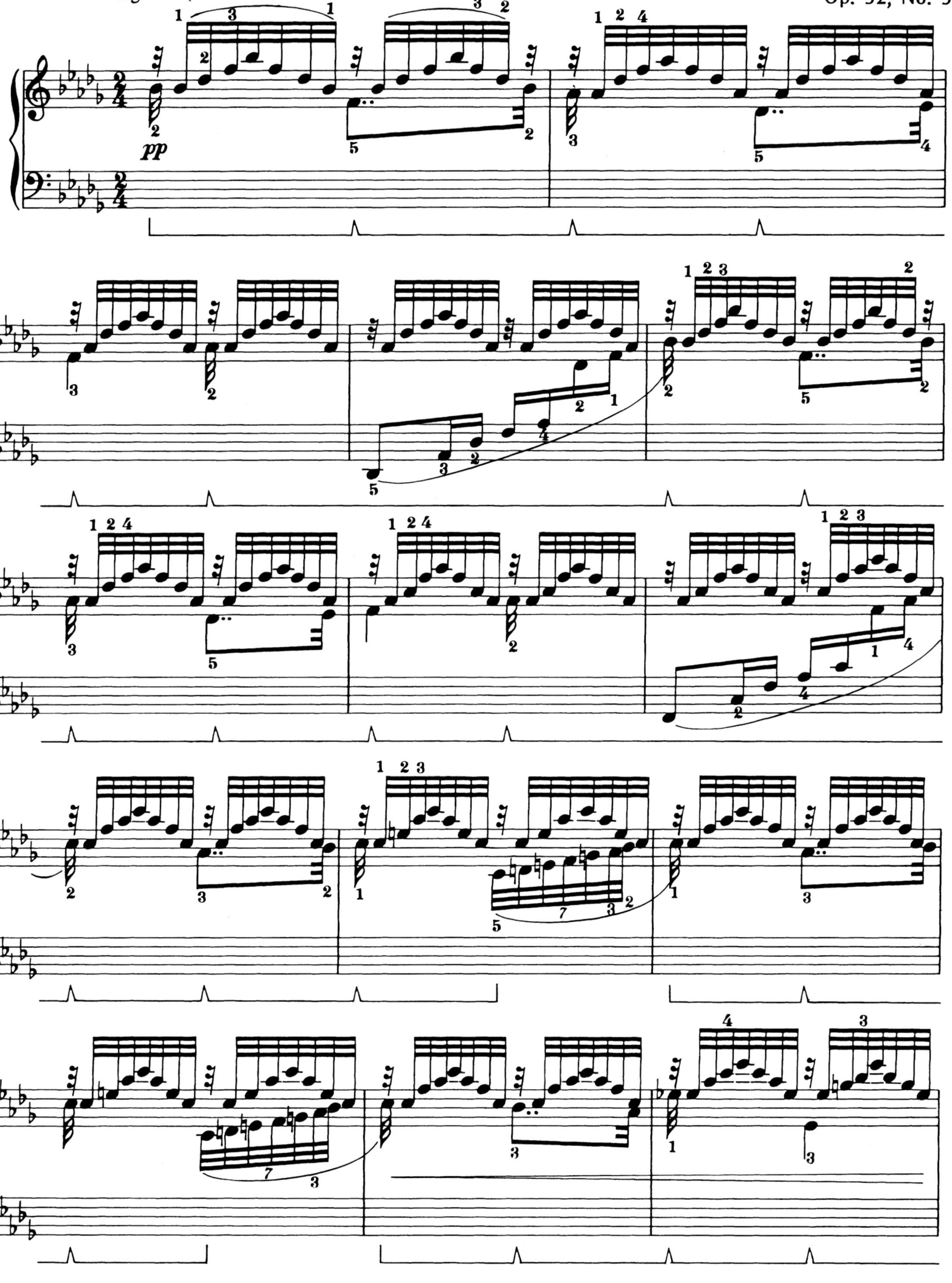

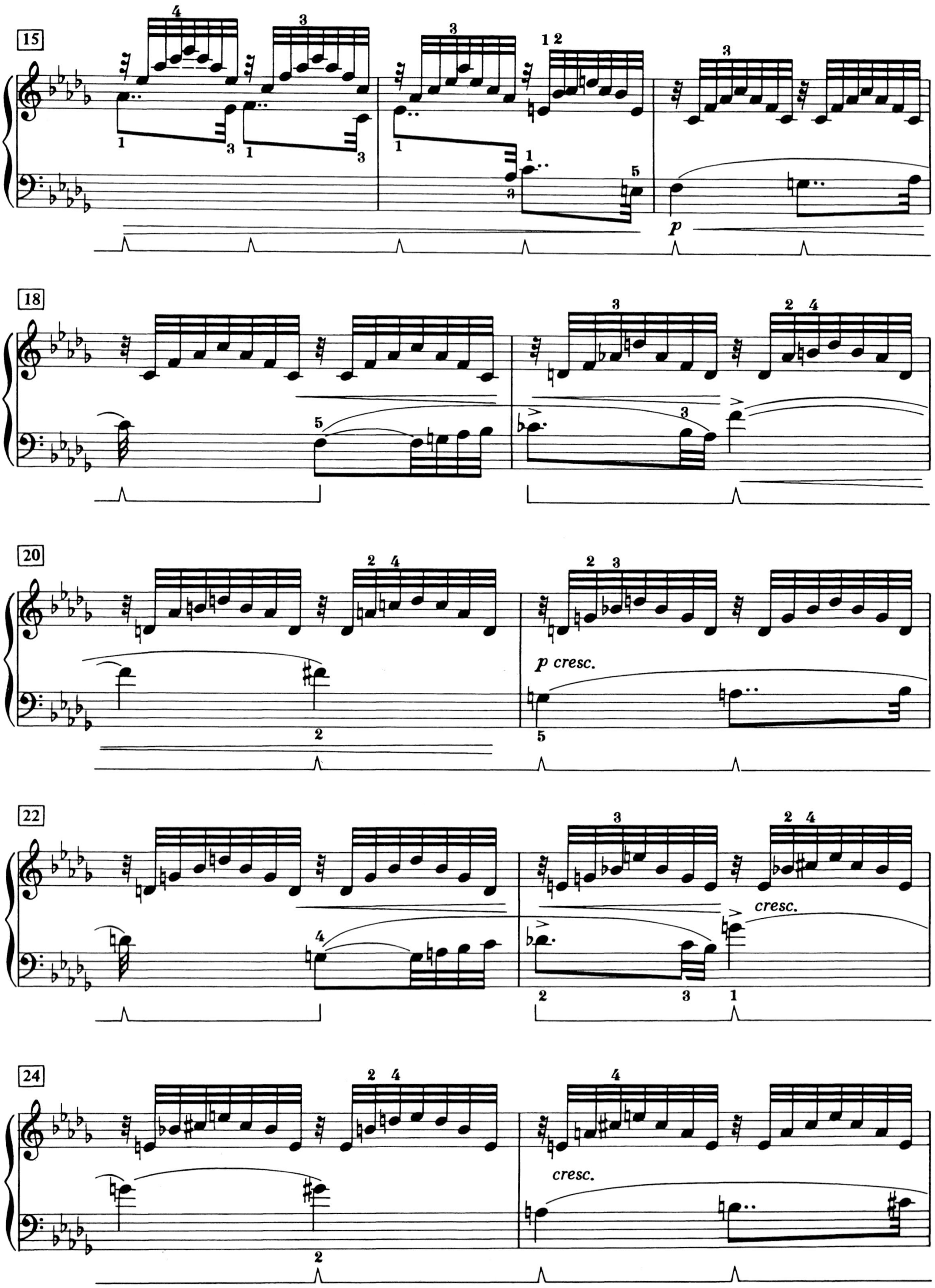
15
18
20
p cresc.
22
cresc.
24
cresc.

26
molto cresc.
28
30
ff
r.h.
33
36
sempre
ff

40
43
fz
46
49
fz
fz
52

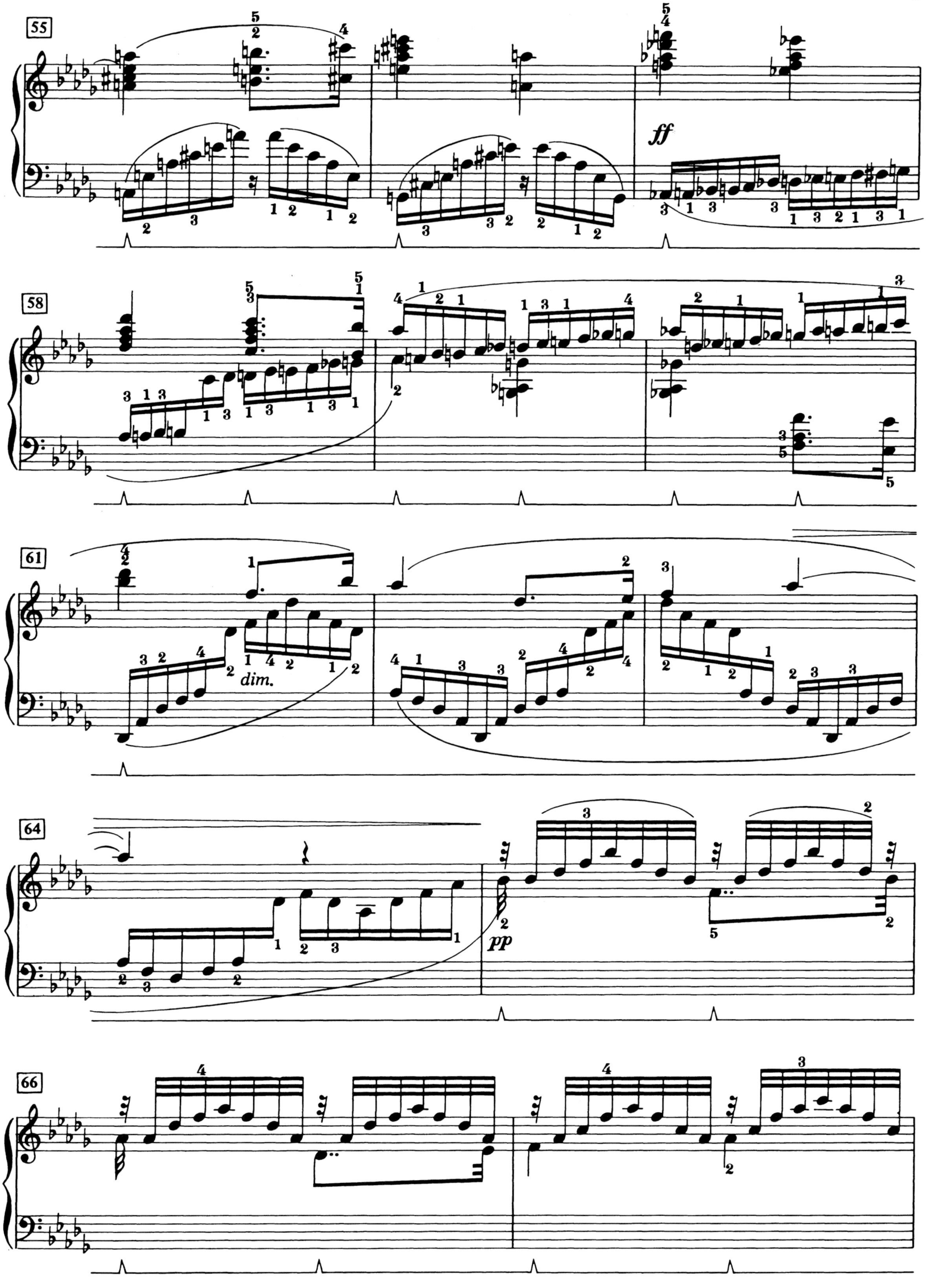
55
ff
58
61
dim.
64
pp
66

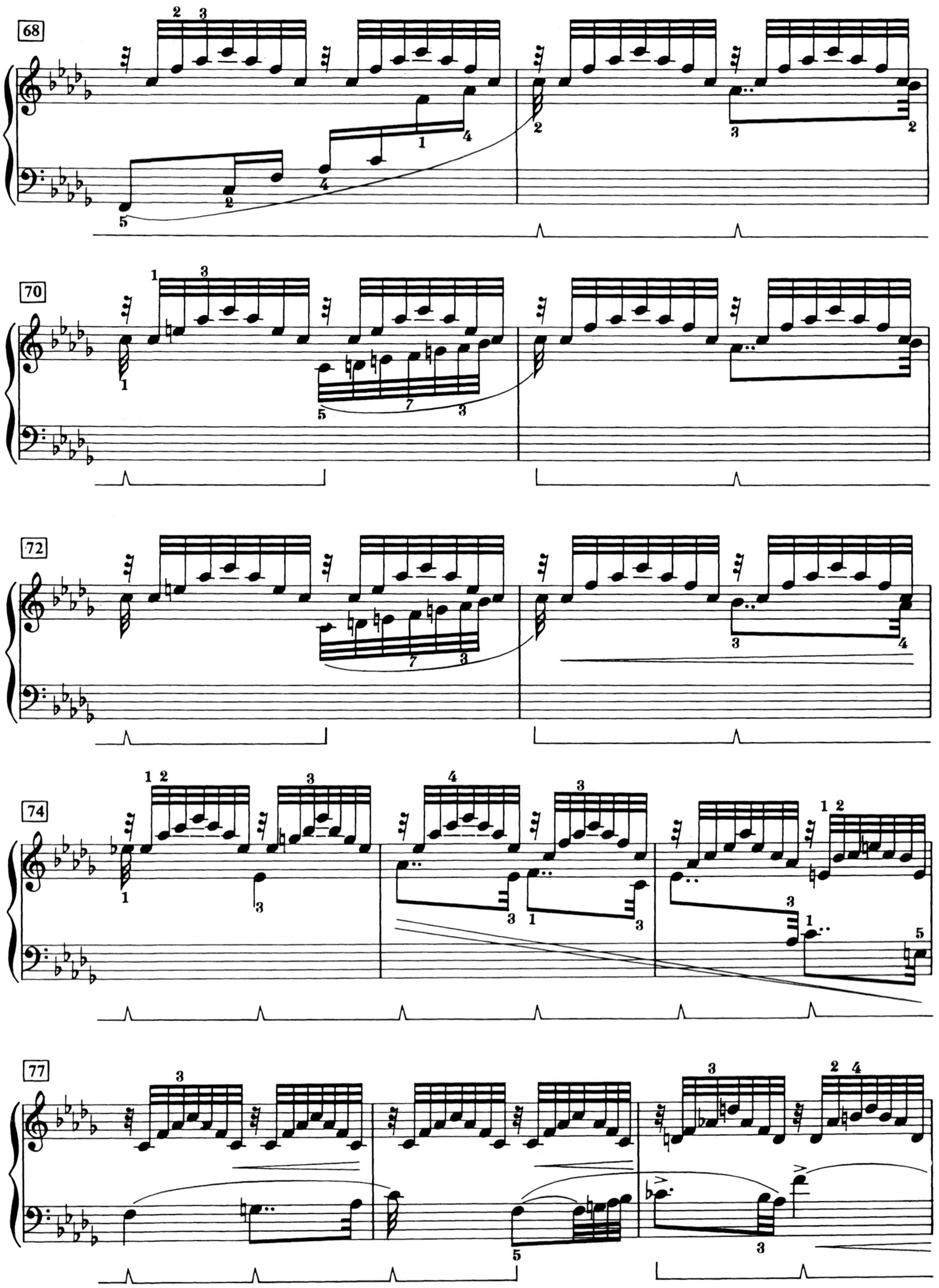

80
82
84
cresc.
86
89
cresc.
ff

ISBN-10: 0-7390-3055-8
ISBN-13: 978-0-7390-3055-4
9 780739 030554
alfred.com
9780739030554
TP
APEX